'When the hurly-burly's done': What's worth fighting for in English Education?

Tony Burgess

Perspectives on English Teaching 1

Series Editor: Viv Ellis

NATE

Perspectives on English Teaching 1

ISBN 0 901291 83 8

© NATE and the authors (2002)

The *Perspectives on English Teaching* series is published by the National Association for the Teaching of English (NATE), the UK subject teacher association for all aspects of the teaching of English from pre-school to university.

NATE
50 Broadfield Road
Sheffield S8 0XJ
e-mail: natehq@btconnect.com
web: www.nate.org.uk

Typeset and printed by Q3 Print Project Management Limited,
Quorn House, Queens Road, Loughborough,
Leics LE11 1HH

Contents

Introduction   1

Talking for Learning; not the whole story
CAROL FOX   5

Literature at Key Stage 3; its place in the classroom
JOAN GOODY   15

Writing, English Teachers and the New Professionalism
TONY BURGESS   25

Contributors   40

Introduction

NATE has a proud tradition of publishing pamphlets by key thinkers in the field of English teaching. A cursory glance at members' bookshelves will reveal slim volumes by Myra Barrs, Harold Rosen, Graham Frater, Pat D'Arcy, Andrew Stibbs and many, many others including, of course, many of the Association's age-range and specialist committees. Sometimes published jointly with the National Association of Advisers in English and sometimes solely by NATE, these short, economically produced publications have been widely distributed and, often, have had an effect upon the development of the profession that belies their humble presentation.

This pamphlet marks the beginning of a new series of NATE publications: *Perspectives on English Teaching*. In the tradition of NATE pamphlets, they will offer individual perspectives on important issues or questions about our lives and work as teachers of English and literacy across the phases. They will be topical and available at little cost to members and will give voice to and stimulate the conversations we have about who we are and what we do. They are not intended to be definitive statements from authorities even though the authors will undoubtedly have great expertise and an authoritative voice. They should be received in the same manner that they are presented: a contribution to an ongoing conversation or an opening move, a work-in-progress or perhaps, occasionally, a personal grumble. They are an expression of NATE's renewed commitment to the development of a professional culture of English teaching.

We are extremely grateful to the distinguished and long-standing members who have contributed to this publication. All three were invited speakers at a NATE regional conference in Brighton in June 2001. The title of that conference is the title of this pamphlet. We wanted to reflect on what we knew to be good English and literacy teaching, on the principles that underlie these practices and to consider how we are positioned by current national strategies and interventions. The conference was promoted with the slogan 'no workshops, no books to plug, no demonstrations of how to comply with the latest initiative.' I admit to fearing that the four of us would be on our own with more tea and biscuits than we could manage while the region's NATE members lay prone on Brighton beach. Very, very reassuringly, I was wrong. The conference attracted a group of 35 teachers on one of the sunniest Saturdays of the year. What I did notice, however, was that I had hardly ever seen them at a local NATE event before.

In the plenary, I plucked up the courage to ask the following question to the floor: 'If we had planned a conference that showed you how to deliver the most recent initiative, would you have come?' The answer was a resounding 'no'. These teachers wanted to attend something that allowed them to listen, read, talk and reflect without responding to someone else's agenda; they wanted to participate in a conference that allowed them to confer. It was this experience, clarified and rationalised through the deliberations of NATE's Management Committee, that led directly to establishing this new *Perspectives* series.

Three inter-related ideas are developed through *When the hurly-burly's done*. The first is that there is a body of knowledge and set of practices related to the teaching and learning of English, that there are insights and voices from within the profession that should and do guide our experience. This is what we hold on to amidst the hurly-burly. Once, they may have been alive at the front of our minds, perhaps during our initial teacher education; lately, they may have been smothered beneath a suffocating discourse of accountability. These ideas are a collective memory that shapes our profession and stimulates the kind

2

of empowering and creative English work to which we aspire. Our own personal knowledge, practices, insights and voices are inextricably bound up with them as are those of our students. This is what provides us with an identity as teachers of English and literacy, something which, when activated, gives us confidence, direction and pleasure. At the heart of it all, as Carol Fox suggests in her essay on talk, is a view of learning that is interactive and social, that 'leaves room for the unforeseen', the development of new knowledge. We ignore all this at our peril.

Second, as a profession we engage with change as an inevitable and necessary process. Rather than swinging between the either/or poles erected by policy-makers and indulging in a barricades rhetoric of them and us, we develop our own new positions and represent them with the confidence lent to us by our professional knowledge. In the specific context of the KS3 English Framework, this is what Tony Burgess refers to in his essay as a new synthesis of research traditions that focus on process and learning with those that give more explicit attention to the forms of language. This synthesis leads to an understanding of English and literacy pedagogy as accretive and differentially emphasised, an understanding that has been debated in recent meetings between QCA and NATE. In other words, we allow ourselves to be more complex than we are required to be.

And thirdly, the time is probably long past when it became necessary to build a new professional culture of English teaching. This strategic move from within the profession and, particularly, from NATE is long overdue. If, for example, we simply follow the rhetoric of the Teacher Training Agency (in its efforts to deal with an unprecedented crisis of teacher recruitment and retention) and conceive of teachers as short-term delivery mechanisms – in the profession for maybe three years and then off to 'something else' – then we identify ourselves as civil service functionaries in a national, supposedly neutral system. In this model, new recruits pick up their script and box of transparencies as they leave their course of training, turn on the overhead projector and perform the delivery. Satisfaction in so far as it is sought comes from observing the shape of the lesson and the

3

regularity of the children's responses. This is a model – crudely cari- catured, I admit – utterly at odds with that demonstrated by Joan Goody in her essay on reading and literature at Key Stage 3. Joan talks of the responsiveness, the responsibility and creativity exercised in good English teaching and how important it is that difficulty and difference are not erased in the pursuit of 'meeting' nationally prescribed objectives.

These ideas are part of the culture of post-war English teaching that the contributors to this pamphlet have both reflected and helped to shape; ideals we would wish to retain and re-develop. The articula- tion of a professional identity that arises from a new strategic positioning is not easy and raises many difficult questions, among the most important being the integrity of the synthesis of traditions and how our view of learning relates to who we think we are as teachers of English. NATE has an important role in this process and we hope that this series, this pamphlet will be a useful starting point.

Viv Ellis

Vice Chair
NATE

Talking for Learning; not the whole story

CAROL FOX

Over the last forty years the uses of speaking and listening for teaching and learning have generated as much passion and controversy among English teachers as those familiar disputed areas of literacy, such as reading with real books, phonics, the importance of spelling and so on. Feelings have always run high, not only because of the crucial relationship between talk and learning but also because of the ways in which the speech styles of different groups of people have traditionally been accorded high or low status in English culture. As I write this piece I am surrounded by books and pamphlets accumulated on my shelves over the years and am reminded of the enormous amount of intellectual energy that we have expended on every aspect of talk – and *talk* was the preferred term pre-National Curriculum – led largely by a relatively small band of English teacher-educators based at the Institute of Education in London together with members of the newly formed London Association for the Teaching of English, (afterwards NATE), whose ranks were later joined by contributors from practitioners outside the profession – psycholinguists, sociolinguists and ethnographers among them. There were major and consistent themes coursing through these exciting and excitable projects, meetings and publications, and I would like to remember and review some of those before considering where we are now, what we might be in danger of losing and what we really must fight to keep. My outline sketch must necessarily be both reductively selective and brief, and really there is a need for a much more extensive account.

The first major impact that I recall came from Chomsky's work in the 1950s and 60s, (though it was not until the early Seventies that I remember its impact on English teaching). Initially the notion that we are all mentally programmed to learn our native language(s) with ease and without instruction well before the age of 5, regardless of differences in intelligence or environment, was liberating in its democratic implications. We could safely assume a kind of equality in language learning competencies, a basis for learning in school that could be the foundation for every child to achieve his or her linguistic and intellectual potential. Transformational linguistics also taught us that children learned by internalising grammatical regularities and applying them by hypothesis testing, whether or not the grammatical features acquired were those of standard or non-standard varieties of the native tongue (Chomsky 1957, 1965). As a Londoner I remember the remarkable impact of reflecting on the *grammar of cockney*, or, later, after I had been teaching a little while, of Caribbean Creoles and dialects, for I had been brought up to believe that only standard English was grammatical – a persistent idea that has not fully retreated from the education system. However, Chomsky demonstrated his theory on 'idealised' samples of language rather than the imperfect speech that we all actually utter, and teachers were well aware that however liberating the new grammar was, schools were places of astonishing diversity and that differences, rather than similarities, in pupils' speech were at the forefront of their concern. Sociolinguists extended the notion of competence to include actual utterances and interactions – *communicative competence* was born. The ability to know what to say, and how and when and whether to say it became an abiding concern in both the theory and practice of English teaching. Major sociolinguistic studies of language learning by the British linguists Wells and Halliday published in the 1970s and 80s uncovered for us the importance of interaction between adults and children in the early years (Wells et al. 1979; Halliday 1975); those concerns are still central to the modern National Curriculum for English. However, even as communicative competence was being conceptualised by Hymes (1970) and others, the idea that language was solely a *communicative* tool was up for examination.

6

The work of Vygotsky was first made available in translation in the 1960s and studied and disseminated by James Britton until he died in the 1990s. *Mind in Society* did not come until the late 70s; it was *Thought and Language* (1962) that made the major impact on English teachers. Interestingly, although Vygotsky's experiment on the formation of scientific concepts was central to the book, his ideas took longer to reach other subject areas. The Vygotskyan claim that at the onset of language the routes of language and thought became inextricably intertwined and mutually interdependent made us reconsider the role of talk in our classrooms. A silent classroom, once so desirable and the mark of a teacher's control over things, was seen to be wasteful of pupils' natural capacity to learn by talking things through. It was not only Vygotsky's social theories of learning and language that drove the new emphasis on talk. The situation of our practice in school, particularly in the inner cities, was also forcing changes – comprehensivisation, mixed ability groupings, the arrival of pupils from the Caribbean and other parts of the world in the 1950s and 60s – the sheer diversity of the children facing us in the classroom challenged the traditional ways of doing things.

In some places, lessons where the teacher effectively controlled children's talk from the front of the class gave way to looser structures; working together in small groups pupils were now encouraged to talk through ideas, problems, responses with their peers. Tape recorders appeared in classrooms. Many of us began to make recordings of children's talk, to transcribe them (a laborious and time-consuming task) and to study exactly what was going on. Some of us were shocked to discover how intrusive and dominating we ourselves were when we were present in the groups, even when we did not want to be and thought we were being sensitive and enabling, and how much more thoughtful and lively the talk could be when we left the children alone with the tape recorder. Sinclair and Coulthard (1975) had shown us that most lessons were dominated by the crude Initiate/Respond/Feedback (IRF) interactional structure and we were desperate to break away from it. Of course many teachers had always encouraged children to talk their thinking aloud, particularly when there were specific problems with identifiable solutions to work out, but now we began to discover the liberating effects of our own absence on what children felt they could say expressively, what they were willing to reveal about themselves, how small group interactions worked.

In the third edition of *Language, the Learner and the School*, originally published in 1969 and then revised in 1986, James Britton considers several transcripts of small group talk by secondary pupils. He shows clearly how children can negotiate together the solution of a particular problem, such as some Latin translation or an experiment in science, how the exchange of ideas can move them all forward. I do not think that this has been lost from current curricula; indeed the myriad ways of using talk for this kind of learning are very explicitly set out in the National Curriculum for English (1989/1995) and in the National Literacy Strategy (Primary NLS 1997; Key Stage 3 Strategy 2001). As Britton points out, such interactions have very clear functions and purposes and the learning outcomes can be defined. But he also presents a transcript of a different kind, where a group of boys with their teacher are discussing things closer to home – their parents, education, life opportunities and so on. There is a kind of unstated consensus running beneath much of what is said and Britton carefully analyses where the signs of implicit agreement break through. Commenting that the talk does not move from the expressive to the referential, that a kind of unspoken agreement about things between the boys never gets really challenged, Britton discusses the importance of the kind of interactions where we might see things from somebody else's point of view and thereby possibly adjust or change our own, and he draws attention to the *implicit meanings* often underlying the children's exchanges:

'we need to bear in mind the possibility that a satisfactory understanding may be reached, in ways that we do not yet understand, by the handling of implicit rather than explicit meanings'.

(Britton 1986 p. 120)

He goes on to suggest that the ways in which teachers learn to handle exploratory, expressive talk are a major part of what teaching and learning to teach is. He warns against too many pre-determined inputs and outputs in designing the curriculum because we run the risk of excluding students' own unforeseen contributions to the learning that takes place. While talk for learning has a firm and important place (even though it has been recast as Speaking and Listening) in the current National Curriculum, we may now be in a position where the kind of exploration Britton wanted us to continue cannot really take place; inputs and outputs are all. It is less usual now to see teachers in their everyday practice making recordings of small group exploratory talk; the sheer business and over-structured nature of the coverage curriculum makes it virtually impossible to do and that is certainly a real loss. However, it is still common for under-graduate students and teachers on various kinds of in-service courses, higher degrees and so on, to study children's language inter-actions and to learn a great deal from them.

In a recent article in *The Guardian* the novelist Ian McEwan sets out more eloquently and movingly than I can the contradictions and gains and losses of what he calls *'the internal exile of social mobility, particularly when it is through the layered linguistic density of English class'*. What he is talking about is the other issue that generated as much passion as the pursuit of talk for learning – the matter of Standard and non-standard varieties of English or, as McEwan puts it *'the mother tongue I've spent most of my life unlearning'* (McEwan 2001). Again there was much tape-recording of real speech by very diverse groups of speakers. In Britain Harold Rosen (1972), and in the US William Labov (1969, 1972), argued for the rich qualities of non-standard speech, for its capacity to represent complex ideas in subtle ways as well as for the expressive qualities more traditionally accorded to dialects. Linguists like Peter Trudgill (1975) argued that personal, regional and social identities were intimately tied into our ideolects and dialects. The issues continue to constitute a battleground in which some contradictory forces are at work. On the one hand we have remained aware that, as the Bullock Report (1975) so famously put it, no child should be required to leave his/her language behind at the school gates. Accordingly the National Curriculum gives scope for the study of different language varieties in school, particularly the appropriateness of this or that form for this or that situation. There is a commendable aim that children should not be disempowered by not knowing the most appropriate form for the situation. Non-standard varieties of course are part of literature as well and there is room there for some exploration and, more importantly, valuing of them. However, the injunction to teach standard spoken English is firm and unequivocal and by the later key stages is a criterion by which speaking and listening are to be assessed. This is of course meant to be underpinned by the layers of grammar teaching that run through the earlier key stages in English. Theoretically children will now be aware of different grammatical constructions and be able to apply them appropriately to their own writing and speech. The recent major emphasis on literacy, which may at first seem to devalue speaking and listening, could help enormously in children's development of and familiarity with standard English if it is perceived that it is largely through literacy that non-standard speakers add the standard to their linguistic repertoires. Ian McEwan while setting out all the personal and social difficulties of losing his mother tongue also argues that there was an important gain in *a fruitful, or at least usefully problematic relationship with an adopted language*. He describes a hesitancy, a scrupulousness, an unsureness with this adopted language which has helped to characterise his prose. But the issue of whether children can or will want to code-switch from situation to situation (as many of us do) is an area that has been fudged. And what applies to children also applies to teachers. Many teachers begin their careers speaking with regional accents, often with some persistent non-standard grammatical features. In my area of the south-east this issue gives rise to anxiety about the entry of potential students to initial teacher education courses and the reception of young teachers in local schools. On the one hand it is not only undesirable but also discriminatory to exclude non-standard speakers from entry to the profession; on the other hand they may be discriminated against in schools and will certainly have to monitor the progress in standard spoken English of their pupils.

The issue of the relationship between Standard English and non-standard varieties is closely connected to the earlier issue I raised in

10

this piece. The kind of small-group, exploratory expressive talk that many of us recorded and thought about in the years before the National Curriculum would take place in the language that children felt comfortable and relaxed with. This was not necessarily the language of the street, playground or football pitch. A glance at the transcripts offered by Britton referred to above, or at the many transcripts that have appeared in the *English and Media Magazine*, the publications of the National Oracy Project, or the seminal and ongoing work of the Centre for Language in Primary Education (CLPE) will confirm that. Children knew they were being recorded, the teacher was often sitting with them and would later listen in to the conversation. Caribbean children, for example, certainly would not speak in the Creoles that in those days were their mother tongues. But they trusted their teachers enough to know that the forms of their speech were not being monitored for the features of standard English, that the teacher was interested in what they had to say and how they interacted in and as a group. It was their meanings that were important and the process of making those meanings explicit, bringing thought into linguistic shape.

An aspect of talk that received great attention from the 1970s onwards was storytelling. In his work on non-standard varieties of American English Labov used his respondents' ability to relate a spontaneous narrative to demonstrate their linguistic skill and complexity and to argue against the proposal that working-class speakers were often confined to speaking a 'restricted code' (Bernstein 1971). He also demonstrated very clearly the importance of the kind of trust that comes from informality in the methodology used to elicit his subjects' stories. In our study of learning to read the importance of story was seen to be paramount by Meek and others (1974), but now a strong link was made with spoken language. Harold Rosen (1984) argued strenuously that narrative was the common, taken-for-granted everyday form by which we thought, learned and communicated and that storytelling should be taken seriously. Betty Rosen (1990) demonstrated the enormous potential of storytelling to inspire disaffected teenagers in a London secondary school, and, later, the National Oracy Project (1988–91) gave great attention and prominence to storytelling as a way of developing spoken language and actually discovering what pupils were capable of. I made my own contribution to this with a study of the spontaneous storytelling of pre-school children and the great impact made on their narratives by the literature that had been read to them (Fox 1993). A look at recent books on oracy shows that storytelling still receives a great amount of attention from those who are interested in children's spoken language. Throughout the later decades of the twentieth century narratologists had taught us a great deal about story structures both in speech and writing and it became possible to look at stories more systematically. We could analyse them and describe them in ways that were not so accessible with the tricky and complex structures of informal conversations among groups of talkers, the kinds of conversations that so interested Britton. Interestingly too, oral stories do not necessarily benefit from a strict emphasis on standard language but often take their life and colour from non-standard usage as Labov and others have shown us over the years.

During the decades that I have been remembering here a major theme, one that has the power to bring together the aspects of talk under discussion, has been the relationship between language and power. This has been present in much of the work that has been done on exploratory small-group talk, on the relationship of standard English to non-standard, on the importance and commonality of storytelling and on other major movements in English too – work with bilingual pupils for example, or the application of theories about genre and register (which can be traced back to the sociolinguistic work of Halliday and others in the 1970s). We have been made anxious about the 'long tail of underachievement', concerned to empower the still large numbers of pupils who do not succeed in the education system, hopeful that making all aspects of English knowledge available to all will change things. So the following are some of the broad principles I would want us to keep:

- continue to open up the opportunities for children to learn by talking to one another and sharing their knowledge and thinking to

12

generate new knowledge and new thinking – and continue to tape-record and study this kind of talk, including our own role in it;

- take seriously the implications for many children of their linguistic situation in a still class-divided society, teaching explicitly about the relationship of language and power and the relative status of different language varieties;
- continue to recognise that the most powerful route to the mastery of Standard English is through long, satisfying and consistent experience of the special languages of literacy and literature;
- make space for children to tell the stories that will give voice to their own unique social, linguistic and individual experiences.

Defining what can be learned, known and tested, split up into functions, purposes, audiences and situations, planned for in specific time-slots and followed up by clearly delineated practices, all of these do not amount to the whole story. Britton emphasises the importance of mutual *trust* between teacher and learner, the *negotiation* of meanings within the security of that trust, an interactive and social view of learning that will have room for the unforeseen pupils' knowledge to be formulated and to develop. It is in the consideration of talk for learning that these emphases emerge. The danger of national curricula and strategies is to imagine that the research on classroom language has been done, that we know where we ought to be going and that these complex aspirations can be achieved if we simply prescribe the talk situations and ensure the practice. Whereas in fact we were only beginning to learn where talk for learning could take us at the inception of the National Curriculum for English.

References

Barnes, D., Britton, J. and Rosen, H. (1969) (First ed) *Language, the Learner and the School* Harmondsworth: Penguin

Barnes, D., Britton, J. and Torbe, M. (1986) (Third ed) *Language, the Learner and the School* Harmondsworth: Penguin

Bernstein, B. (1971) *Class, Codes and Control* Vol. 1, London: Routledge and Kegan Paul

Bullock, A. et al. (1975) *A Language for Life* London: HMSO

Chomsky, N. (1957) *Syntactic Structures* Cambridge, Mass.: MIT Press

Chomsky, N. (1965) *Aspects of the Theory of Syntax* Cambridge Mass: MIT Press

DfEE (1999) *The National Curriculum for England: English* London: QCA/HMSO

Fox, C. (1993) *At the Very Edge of the Forest* London: Cassell

Halliday, M. A. K. (1975) *Learning How to Mean* London: Edward Arnold

Hymes, D. (1970) 'On Communicative Competence' in *Sociolinguistics* J. B. Pride and J. Holmes (eds) Harmondsworth: Penguin 1973

Labov, W. (1969) 'The Logic of Non-Standard English' in *Georgetown Monographs on Language and Linguistics* Vol. 22:1–31, Washington DC: Georgetown University Press

Labov, W. (1972) *Language in the Inner-City* Oxford: Basil Blackwell

McEwan, I. (2001) 'Mother Tongue' in *The Guardian* (*Review*): 1–3, October 13th

Meek, M., Warlow, A. and Barton, G. (1974) *The Cool Web* Oxford: The Bodley Head

Rosen, B. (1990) *And None of it was Nonsense* London: Mary Glasgow

Rosen, H. (1972) *Language and Class: a critical look at the theories of Basil Bernstein* Bristol: The Falling Wall Press

Rosen, H. (1984) *Stories and Meanings* Sheffield: NATE

Sinclair, J. and Coulthard, M. (1975) *Towards an Analysis of Discourse* Oxford: Oxford University Press

Trudgill, P. (1975) *Accent, Dialect and the School* London: Edward Arnold

Vygotsky, L. (1962) *Thought and Language* Cambridge Mass: MIT Press

Vygotsky, L. (1978) *Mind in Society* Cambridge, Mass: Harvard University Press

Wells, G., Montgomery, M. and Maclure, M. (1979) 'Adult-Child Discourse: outline of a model of analysis' *Journal of Pragmatics* 3: 337–380

Literature at Key Stage 3 : its place in the classroom

JOAN GOODY

As a teacher who started in the classroom in the early Fifties, my aim is to look back and consider what I most want to retain in the field of reading and literature as we are rushed into a most controversial change of direction and emphasis in the teaching of English. I don't want to be in danger of seeming to be harking back nostalgically to some mythical good old days, so I should explain straightaway that the points I want to make refer as much to what many of us have worked towards, have tried to develop, as to what we have actually achieved. I am focusing, loosely, on Key Stage 3, not only for the obvious reasons, but also because in the days I am referring to there were no national tests or exams to confine one's work, until year 11; and English departments and individual teachers were entrusted with the selection of texts for their particular classes, and ways of approaching them and responding to them.

The classroom experience I am drawing on includes a secondary modern school in the Fifties, two ethnically mixed inner-city comprehensives in the creative (or permissive?) Sixties through to the cuts of the mid-Seventies, and then advisory work with the ILEA English and multi-ethnic teams, which included working with teachers in a variety of classrooms. Since retirement, towards the end of the Eighties, I have had the opportunity to visit classrooms on a regular basis as a governor in a school with a particularly high proportion of refugee children (this included two years working under Special Measures). I have also had contact recently with classrooms across the country through NATE'S International/ Multicultural Literature Project, where project members monitored

15

their classroom experience as they introduced – or extended the use of – multicultural literature in their schools (see the two NATE publications *Opening New Worlds* and *Multicultural Literature in the Classroom*).

What I most want to hang on to, and am most afraid of losing, is our belief in the power, and place, of imaginative literature in the classroom, in learning. This is what I would most worry about if I was still teaching English.

However, to expose children effectively to the literature, as well as to all the other aspects of English teaching, we need the freedom, the time, to pay attention to the classroom context, the learning environment. For that too, already affected by the English Curriculum, is further threatened by the spanking pace, rigid planning and tight organisation demanded by the Framework, by the insistence on teaching from the front.

It is crucial to be able to retain and develop a positive attitude towards the diversity which exists in every classroom, to be able to allow for the fact that children come to the classroom with varied experiences, histories, home backgrounds and outlooks, abilities and disabilities, aptitudes and interests. We need to be free to acknowledge, in the way we organise our teaching, the different starting points of young people and their many routes of learning, particularly, but not only, in the multicultural, multilingual classroom. We need to be able to see the diversity that students bring to the classroom as ultimately enriching, as forming part of the resources that stimulate the teaching and learning of all. In more practical terms we need the time to make the classroom welcoming and safe – where there is a place for children's own cultures, traditions and values, and where young people can learn how to work together creatively and collaboratively, can talk frankly and listen to each other, and have opportunities to formulate their thoughts and to reflect. We as teachers need to be relaxed enough to listen to our students as individuals and to enter into discussion with them. All this takes time, slows down the pace, but we very soon reap the benefits.

Although I know the 'class novel' was already on its way out in some schools before the advent of the Framework, and extracts were taking over, what I most want to retain, or regain, is the unifying experience of reading a whole novel with a class – to give them, each individual, the experience of sustained in-depth reading; to have time to read all, or most of, particular novels aloud so that whatever stage of competence in reading individual students have reached, they can all become imaginatively involved and *have access to the literary experience*, be exposed to the full impact of the writing.

For me, Key Stage 3 is the time to concentrate on the experience of reading, to engage with reading, and to encourage and value the felt response, whether this is in writing or talk, or role play or drama. The students take part in the unfolding of the story, and bring to it something of themselves, so that reading a familiar novel with a new class is a fresh experience for the teacher. I remember that with an old favourite of mine, Rosemary Sutcliffe's *The Eagle of the Ninth* (where the three central characters are Marcus, a young Roman centurion serving in Britain and searching for his father's lost legion; Esca, his personal slave, who is British; and Cottia, also British, who rebels against her family's efforts to make her conform to the Roman way of life), it was the students themselves, those from the Caribbean in particular, who brought home to me how relevant and thought-provoking the book was for a culturally mixed class, reflecting as it did, in the removed setting of Roman-occupied Britain, aspects of their own situations and problems, validating their experience; and this opened up new ways of looking at the novel and enriched their responses. Two responses that remain in my mind are a play written by a Jamaican boy about a British family feeling resentful about the Romans trying to change their way of life – with as the climax the daughter 'going out' with a Roman soldier; and a girl of mixed race who is able for the first time not only to write, but to talk to the class, about how it felt to be told by her white grandparents to pretend she was from Cyprus, not the Caribbean.

I couldn't have planned ahead mechanistically, fitting in the listed objectives from the Framework, and asked them to withdraw from their involvement in order to generalise about the author's craft – although we would have wanted to look at some of the writing closely, of course. And I certainly couldn't use the story to teach grammatical structures or define parts of speech. On the other hand a novel that imaginatively involves the readers (and listeners) acts as a powerful language model, and extends and refines their own use of language. The students are receptive to the structures and registers and conventions of the written language, which will now be in the framework of their expectations in their own further reading; and their familiarity increases the range of possibilities for them to draw on in their own writing. In this shared response to a book, the students seem to have little difficulty in understanding language that may be different, or maybe more complex than they are used to; they are able to take on different styles of writing. And they acquire new vocabulary naturally, in context. We can build on all this. It is helpful for all the students including those who are learning English as an additional language, and those who may be inexperienced in using standard forms of English.

The special scope and function of the novel for young people growing up, and their response to it, may seem all too obvious to us ourselves, but because this whole area tends to be neglected in both the English Curriculum and the Framework we need to re-state it. We are told that it's missing from the Framework because teachers already do it well! But where is the time for it now? How will teachers new to the profession take it on, if their school is working strictly to the Framework?

In all sorts of ways students are trying to get their bearings in life around them, and to make sense of the wider world, but they don't have time to reflect, to see clearly, in the rushed overcrowded lives many of them lead. They need that special quality of the novel that enables them to stand back and look calmly at a limited, manageable circle or slice of life that is outside themselves, and yet is directly accessible to them through empathy with the characters, and through other significant links they may have with the theme or setting of the novel, as individuals or as a class.

18

Through a range of carefully chosen literature, and their responses to it, young people examine human relationships and confront moral dilemmas; they are able to explore aspects of their roots and heritages (their own and other people's – including dual and cross-cultural heritages); they are able to take on other people's perspectives; they construct images and interpretations of the world, which help to dispel some of the confusion, frustration and uncertainty they so often feel about their place in it. Aspects of other subject areas are brought to life, and their significance and interdependence revealed; and literature is a powerful medium and resource for important elements of the Citizenship syllabus, in particular, of course, for 'spiritual, moral, social and cultural development'.

The students share the common experience but may branch out in their responses to it, following their particular concerns and working, probably with guidance, at their own levels. A discussion about *Tell Freedom* by Peter Abrahams, between three fourteen-year-olds, encapsulates for me some of the possibilities we need to hold on to in our work. The book is an imaginative and very positive retelling of the author's life story up to the age of about twenty, in pre-Mandela South Africa, and reads like an autobiographical novel. It evokes vividly his harsh childhood, his struggle to get himself an education and the effects of this on his whole life; and eventually his reflections on Christianity, and on Marxism as a possible solution.

The boys became very involved with the book and finished it quickly on their own (but were keen to participate in the class reading, too). They had been chatting about elements of the story and asked to borrow the tape recorder so that they could have a focused discussion, and play it back to themselves. First a bit about the boys themselves. Elias (who came from Dominica when he was about nine) had been rather aggressively debating in previous talk about books, and in both talk and writing he tended to follow his own agenda, and would make statements, declaim even, rather than discuss. This time he is relaxed, wanting to discuss *with* the others perhaps because he feels on secure ground, and close to his special interest, the African heritage. Fred is a white boy, with a Spanish mother, and is completely bilingual. You can sense the effect it has on him to be exposed so intimately to Abrahams' experience. He has taken it into his own world view, and thus feels able to talk with the two black boys more confidently than he could have done if the book was set in London. He is alert and open, making positive contributions, and weaving what the others have to say into his own understanding. Tony, who came from St Lucia when he was six, is probably the most competent and is the one who has the greatest insights into the book, but he needs the friendly support of the others to help him to sustain his thinking and formulate his ideas, and they in turn build on this.

The boys are very fluent in their discussion, but at the same time reflective and questioning, and you can see how it helps that they are contributing from different standpoints, but are at ease with each other. The tape is a good example of a sustained response, and of the kind of collaborative, exploratory work I referred to at the beginning of this essay. Throughout the discussion, the boys are loosely anchored to the common experience, the book – not talking about literary qualities but aware of them (they have commented elsewhere on the vivid telling of the story, the portrayal of moving incidents, the evocation of family life and its strains, of street life, the humour, and the author's balanced outlook). They start by describing to themselves the kind of book it is, increasing their familiarity with it. They move onto the whole business of apartheid and discuss calmly how it came about, fitting together what they know and what they can conjecture. From here they go back more closely to the text and take up Lee's (Abrahams') encounters with Christianity and white missionaries, and his experiences of education. They speculate as to why exactly it is that the whites keep the blacks uneducated, and on the position of the educated black South Africans. From here they branch out into South Africa's relationship with the rest of the world, then onto Hitler, Vietnam and Enoch Powell, and finally decide to get back to *Tell Freedom*, to sum up:

> *Fred*: Let's see if we can assemble all this, and you know ...
> *Elias*: That's a good idea.

Tony: Make something out – make something – yeah, all right.

Elias: And construct.

Assemble, make, construct. And so they go back to Lee's childhood.

Tony: ... So Lee, he has a very mixed childhood, very rough child-hood, where he's been passed from one hand to another – doesn't he? So he grows up with a mixture of feeling inside of him, doesn't he.

Fred: Yeah, Lee ...

Tony: You know what I mean – because he sees things from so many views . You know, so – er –

Elias: That's what makes the book so interesting.

And these boys have been able to share that 'mixture of feeling', to 'see things from so many views'. They take this on until they get to Lee's disenchantment with the Stalinists and Trotskyists when vital discussion springs up again ... .

I was tempted to ask them to write up their discussion as an appreci-ation or long review but luckily thought better of it. The discussion, captured on tape, was an end in itself. But the experience of it would help to shape their writing on other books (and on particular issues or aspects they wanted to focus on in writing in this book). They played appropriate parts of the tape to the rest of the class, and some individ-uals insisted on listening to the whole tape.

I have talked about the shared class novel but obviously that is just one aspect of reading. We also need to ensure that the students have time to read together in groups, not only to allow for more choice of texts, but to learn to take charge of their own reading: to take on the responsibility for how they're going to tackle the text together, for deciding as they read what aspects and issues they will want to discuss, and what response they will make in writing or orally to the class, the teacher, or just for themselves. *They* are asking questions here. This is a stage towards becoming a really independent reader.

Group reading is needed, too, to cater for the stages in reading students need to go through, for increasing confidence and fluency, for helping the less competent, or the students who are learning English as an additional language. And time is needed too, to establish sustained individual silent reading, for students have most unequal opportunities at home for this.

Then there is poetry. Poetry is, or needs to become, both commonplace and special. We have to create an established place for it in the classroom. Children and young people become familiar with it as a genre, and not only with reading it but with listening to it, with voicing it, and with writing it themselves. They have to learn to listen (without the text in front of them as will as with it), and to hear it in their heads; and they have to experience voicing it not only to appreciate it, but in order to understand how a new poem might sound, and sometimes how to reveal the meaning. This is not as a performance (that is another matter) but just quietly to themselves, or to each other.

As with prose texts I would want to be able to concentrate on experience, aesthetic experience, rather than analysis and criticism – although criticism develops naturally through discussion – and to expose the students to a range of themes, images, moods, metaphor, sound patterns and effects, and rhythms; to expose them to serious poems and light-hearted ones; and to poems that relate to them implicitly, include them, touch on their experience, their backgrounds and cultural perspectives; and to the those that take them into new areas. I would want to be able to spend time on presenting and exploring certain key poems (chosen probably according to loose English department guidelines and the needs of the particular class) and to introduce others spontaneously at appropriate moments; and to go back to poems, to keep them in circulation, so that the students start to hold them in memory (the ten minutes at the beginning of a lesson, now mainly reserved for spelling was often very useful here!).

We need to keep opportunities open for students to discover poems for themselves (and for others), perhaps motivating them in the first place by asking them to make selections rounds themes and places, and to discuss with each other what to include. Obviously a variety of poetry collections is needed in book boxes and class libraries, and perhaps more important, class collections that can be built up and added to by both students and teachers. There is a particular need for this in culturally mixed schools for although there is plenty of published poetry available these days from the Caribbean, and to a lesser extent from South East Asia and Africa, it is difficult to find enough from the range of cultures now represented in our classrooms. Students' own writing is important here; and parents and community centres have proved helpful, particularly with poetry in the community languages.

When it comes to response in writing I am asking that at this stage young people don't have to distance themselves from the poetry and try to generalise about it. There is so much to be gained from their direct experience. They have to learn early on that you don't 'solve' a poem, that there are layers of meaning that you come to gradually, that you don't have to explain away a poem in order to be able to appreciate it; that what you feel about it can be as important as what you are able to explain. Once this is established they learn from talking together confidently but at the same time tentatively (or reflecting quietly on their own), and perhaps discussing questions devised to guide them, and where appropriate, explaining themselves in writing.

It is this workshop approach to poetry teaching that I want to hold on to, and the flexibility to be able to achieve and enjoy it.

I have stressed here the aspects of reading that I feel most strongly about and it may appear out of proportion looked at apart from the rest of the teaching of English. I have not set out to argue with the Framework or the individual objectives within it; but studying it, and listening to teachers who are working to it, has if anything strengthened my belief in the power of imaginative literature in learning, and its place in the classroom. I do realise that there are things we can all learn from the Framework, and that advisers and literacy consultants are trying to find ways of fitting in what we want to retain. But it should be the other way round: we should be able to retain our responsibility and creativity and be able to make use of the Framework as a substantial checklist and for guidance in areas where we need it.

References

Abrahams, P. (1954) *Tell Freedom* London: Faber
Goody, J. (ed.) (1995) *Opening New Worlds: Explorations in the Teaching of Literature with an International Dimension* Sheffield: NATE
Goody, J. and Thomas, K. (eds) (2000) *Multicultural Literature in the Classroom: Teachers' Accounts of Innovative Work with Years 1 to 5* Sheffield: NATE
Sutcliff, R. (1954) *Eagle of the Ninth* Oxford: Oxford University Press

Writing, English Teachers and the New Professionalism

TONY BURGESS

Writers, young or old, meet intersecting challenges. They must construct text, confront the expectations of their context, struggle for the wording of their meanings. All come together in the act of writing. Integrating these elements in the focus of instruction, and balancing attention between them, is probably perennial as an issue for the teaching of writing in schools.

Before the coming of curriculum movements, texts written by young people in school were mostly locked within traditions of schooling. Curriculum subject teaching and the influence of examinations shaped writing in the secondary schools. The essay tended to be the default option, accompanied by notes and copying and tests, which still form much of writing across the curriculum. In the elementary schools, as the notion of a primary phase of education emerged, progressives began to win attention for young writers' voices and their meanings from copying and imitation and grammar dominated assumptions of the codes, but advance was slow. For more than fifty years, the School Certificate, and subsequently O' level, held the edifice together, with questions and topics for composition, which rarely varied.

Curriculum oriented research, from the Fifties onwards, drew on insights from psychology, anthropology and linguistics, and helped to change the practices of post-war years. Such work promoted a new attention to the writer, and to making meaning in the act of composition. There were major gains in understanding the importance of audience and of the functions of written language. The priority of real writing was stressed, as opposed to writing exercises, accompanied by a focus on the processes of composing and by a widened sense of the variety of texts young writers can attempt. As important, specific attention to writing was supported by more general transformation of understandings about language, including recognition of the part that writing plays in learning and of the different forms of literacy encountered by young people growing up in multilingual as well as monolingual communities. Such gains in understanding derived not just from research but also from initiatives by teachers. Curriculum development owed much to the creative adaptation of research by teachers, working against the background of curriculum subject movements, developing and innovating practice, confronting new conditions in the schools and broader cultural change.

What seems at issue in contemporary discussion concerning principle is the meeting of understandings developed from psychology and anthropology with the challenge of a new focus on the text arising in linguistics. The arguments first surfaced in debates about Sir John Kingman's enquiry into a model of language. They underpin debates about the Key Stage 3 English Framework and to some extent the primary literacy hour. Much will turn, as always, on the creativity of teachers in working with these different theoretical strands. What complicates this process, of discussion and creative adaptation, is the coming of a more directive system. I want to argue here that it is necessary to keep discussion of principle together with a broader reconsideration of professionalism, as we reflect on English teaching's future.

Within new systems of accountability, and emerging versions of the role of the professional, relations between practitioners and research have been fundamentally changed. The issue now confronting English teaching concerns not principle alone but also whether there is room within contemporary management of teaching for a sense of exploration of issues and for discussions that include the legitimate contribution of professional reflection and opinion. The task seems how to move strategically towards establishing a renewed profes-sionalism within a different educational climate. Such considerations

26

look much wider than teaching writing, but I believe that they are ones to which English teachers should attend, and I shall take up points around them towards the close.

To pose the meeting of understandings in contemporary discussion is to recall the richness of the various lines of thought that have helped to shape the practices of English teachers, in post-war years. I believe that it is helpful to take account of three principal directions. These include a person-centred, psychologically oriented concentration on language's role in learning, attention paid to culture, and to difference and variety, deriving ultimately from anthropology, and a changing picture of the forms of the language within linguistics. Behind such concentrations lie broad and many-sided enquiries. Each has been important. Their impact has set writing within a wider framework of ideas and offered general orientations for pedagogy.

A change of emphasis toward writing used in learning forms one such line of argument, deriving from the Vygotsky an inheritance developed by James Britton, from the sixties onwards. In this line of thought, concern with learning language, or with language acquisition, or with development in writing, is integrated into a larger interest in language in the development of mind. Some difficulty perhaps arises from familiarity with this perspective; and the richness of its insights, and their profound intention, is not always grasped in current references to learning or in current commentary. Among the implications that follow is a raising of the stakes for writing instruction to include the part that writing plays in pupils' wider intellectual development, as well as just the skills of written language.

From such as point of view, content in pupils' writing is differently perceived, since the use of language in thinking is seen to lead the acquisition of resources as a writer, not just as a chance accompaniment. Writing's place is altered among the various ways of using language made available in classrooms, since writing figures alongside other language modes, and not as a discrete undertaking. A different weight attaches then to working with what pupils want to say, to the shuttle between experience and talk and reading and

27

writing in the preparation of text, and to the question of what tasks and contexts best promote transactions between pupils and the written word.

Britton's (1975) work on audience and function in the sixties and seventies followed from this concentration on language in the development of mind. He did more than highlight the importance of these components, as dimensions of variety in writing that young writers needed to master and control. He also carried his investigation through to schools, and charted patterns of school writing and school learning. The critical thrust of his enquiry showed closed and open options for writing, which were linked to teaching in school subjects. In some school subjects, an open pattern offered opportunities for work in different functions intended for a range of audience. In others, writing options were confined to classifying and reporting information for an examining audience.

Among the points that Britton raised were whether patterns of this kind sufficiently exploited the power of writing and whether all modes were of equal value in learning. He had a special interest in the potential of what he called expressive writing as a first draft of ideas. In relation to informative writing he raised the issue of abstraction. Following the American writer and philosopher James Moffett, he saw the level of abstraction required as central to the differences within informative writing and stressed the place for speculative and deductive forms in the development of pupil's thinking.

This general perspective, and Britton's work on function and on audience, was disseminated in the seventies through the Bullock Report and through the work of NATE. It was also influential in the States, and was a strand in the American work on process writing in the Seventies and Eighties. In the States, the background was psycholinguistic, and Donald Graves' work on writing processes, and Frank Smith's on reading and writing, rests on a tradition formed from the union between cognitive psychology and linguistics dating from the fifties. At the centre of Graves' (1986) well known work is the writer, learning to control the process, supported by the apparatus of workshops, conferencing and re-drafting that he developed to promote this. Classroom teachers working with Graves, such as Nancy Atwell and Lucy Calkins, carried the development of writing practices further and built on these essential insights. Both Graves's work and Britton's were influential in the American Writing Program, developing from the seventies, in the States, and also in the National Writing Project, here in the Eighties, developed from this model.

Looking back across this psychologically oriented strand, with its emphases on the writer and the learner, on process, and on the priority for the role of language in learning, the danger is that it is simply taken for granted. At its best, the work on writing processes was renewed by steadily accumulating examples and by the advocacy of teachers for the writing that resulted. There was a spirit of enquiry into the effectiveness of student conferences of different kinds and into refining practice. Such energy can come to seem quite distant. This concentration on language and learning gained also from the influence of a second broad movement of ideas. Begun from the American anthropologist and sociolinguist, Dell Hymes, in the Seventies, and carried forward into literacy by Shirley Brice Heath in the Eighties, a new attention was paid to language in society, and to culture, variety and difference.

The work in this tradition also sets out from a wider framework, inviting consideration of writing in the context of more general literacy. As important, literacy is seen not just as individual achievement but as social practices and events in culture and society. Hymes (1972) argued that in thinking about language in society, we needed to be both more general and more specific than was usual in approaching language as a system in conventional linguistics. Greater generality was needed because often more than one language existed in a society, and issues turned on relations between different languages and among bilingual speakers. We needed to be more specific because often people spoke a variant of language, either dialectally or stylistically. The essence of language was diversity, rather than homogeneity. In Brice Heath's (1983) study of different

29

speech communities in South Carolina, she carried forward this approach to literacy. Brice Heath's study showed how different traditions of literacy existed in actual societies and that difficulties could arise in schooling over the transitions between them.

Interest in literacy and culture has been followed in the UK by Brian Street and by a generation of British educational researchers and ethnographers. Hilary Minns (1990) contrasted school literacy with different family literacies in *Read it to me now!* Eve Gregory has contrasted expectations about school literacy in Bangladeshi British communities with actual practices in schools and derived important lessons from this for the teaching of literacy. In her most recent work (2000), with Anne Williams, she delicately describes the different expectations of monolingual and bilingual families, set against traditions in London's east end of taking what was needed from school but not regarding schooled literacy as containing all there is to know. Such ethnographic work has aided teachers in de-centring and de-naturalising the literacy expectations of classrooms and shown the need to make explicit their assumptions about language and about pedagogy, which might otherwise have remained implicit. As broadly psychological and anthropological traditions have come together, it is possible to see a central momentum generated for classroom practices in writing from the meeting between emphases on writing and learning and awareness of the diversity of actual repertoires amongst students.

Inserted into these traditions, it is a focus on the text arising in linguistics that lies behind preoccupations in the current debate. To grasp the impact of this change, it is necessary first to note that interests in text are no less part of earlier concentrations on writing and the writer, though these figure differently. In Britton's work, the concentration on audience and function recognised variety in use of language, as central to the development of young writers. Anthropological researchers placed texts in culture, while pluralising literacy and exploring different literacy traditions. The transition in linguistics has been to focus on texts as well as system in describing language and to remark the writer's (or the speaker's) integration of different language levels in constructing them.

Writing in 1985, in his *Introduction to Functional Grammar*, Halliday puts very clearly his version of the history and the issues.

> 'Twenty years ago, when the mainstream of linguistics was in what has been called its 'syntactic' age, it was necessary to argue against grammar, pointing out that it was not the beginning and the end of all study of language and that one could go a long way towards an understanding of the nature and functions of language without any grammar at all. The authors of the original 'Language in Use' materials produced for the British Schools Council showed that it was possible to produce an excellent language programme for pupils in secondary schools consisting of over a hundred units none of which contained any study of grammar.
>
> Now, however, it is necessary to argue the opposite case, and to insist on the importance of grammar in linguistic analysis. If I now appear as a champion of grammar, it is not because I have changed my mind on the issue but because the issue has changed.'
>
> (Halliday, 1985)

What seems of interest here is the transition in the thinking of linguists, which is indicated in Halliday's remarks. Where in the Sixties, some linguists looked to displace a widely influential concentration on syntax as the object of study, in order to admit awareness above all of the social nature of language, in the eighties issues have changed. While the earlier priority for arguing a wide view of language strengthened understandings about variety and register, the emergence of a new focus has brought new possibilities for integrating the elements of language understandings. The coming of text linguistics has offered a different relevance for attention to the forms of language, with the consequence that the issue of grammar has changed within the picture of language offered from within linguistic studies.

It reveals the central continuity in present debates to look back at the arguments that surfaced round the publication of the Kingman report, in 1988. Part of the brief of this report was to produce a model of the English language to guide the work of teachers, against the background of concern about the teaching of grammar in English and of various, and usually strident, pronouncements about this. Comparing the model produced by Kingman with others at the time takes one quite a long way forwards in representing the implications of different theoretical backgrounds.

Kingman went in for boxes. Briefly, in the Kingman model, the largest box was called the 'forms of language', and this contained an inventory of forms from phonology and morphology, through sentence grammar up to discourse. Three other boxes, much less detailed, covered comprehension and production, acquisition of language and history of language change. Essentially, this was the model of applied linguistics. Aiming to argue against reviving traditional grammar, but also to present the possibility of contemporary language study, a compromise solution was to place an inventory of forms in the foreground, emphasising text as well as word and sentence levels.

NATE, at the time proposed, a different model, with Henrietta Dombey as Chair. NATE picked up the disclaimer offered by Kingman that the boxes could be put in any order and duly put them in a different one. NATE's model emphasised 'the making and understanding of meaning and significance' as central, together with 'language acquisition and development'. In contrast to the lists of Kingman, NATE's model tried to show a dynamic to learning language, in which the making of meaning and development led the acquisition of forms, and awareness of them, influenced in turn by understanding of the social context. It is arguable that the model leaves behind applied linguistics in the process, and shifts to something much more like the Britton focus on learning and the learner, as the creators of the model in NATE were no doubt well aware.

The last part of the story is the model of the Language in the National Curriculum project (LINC). This was produced to underpin the work on knowledge about language, which the project was set up to implement, following the appearance of the earlier report. Here, the model shifts again. Kingman, and applied linguistics, largely disappear. In the centre now is text, flanked by producers and audiences. Text bobs like a cork upon the sea, driven by the winds of the immediate context of situation, while out on the horizon lurk the vast influences of different ideological and institutional systems of society and culture.

LINC's model is essentially the Hallidayan model, it is the model of Norman Fairclough, and the model of critical linguistics. In essential orientation, this is the model of the new secondary English framework, which seeks to build from teaching of the forms, through textual study, towards a critical approach to texts. At the risk of oversimplifying the intentions, it is possible to see a central contrast. In all the Britton work, and in the subsequent American work on process, the focus is on the person using language, on the learner, on the writer. In the anthropological tradition, the focus is similarly on the person, learning different literacies. Texts figure, but are subordinate to a wider developmental perspective. In the model from the new linguistics, the focus is on text. You do not exclude these other traditions by such a focus, but you begin to implement a further hierarchy of considerations for pedagogy, and this where the room is needed for discussion and for the creativity of practice to breathe.

The right approach is surely synthesis. It is not impossible to conceive a practice that attends to the kinds of modelling and to the more explicit forms of instruction that are proposed through concentrating on text, but does not neglect attention to the writer or to wider cultural considerations concerning literacy. A practice that incorporated new understandings concerning texts would be strengthened by continuing recognition of old questions concerning how young people work at what they want to say and what tasks and contexts best promote their writing. It would be a loss to English teaching if at the point of seeking to implement new strategies and practices too much emphasis were placed on contrast with past practice rather than on continuity. We should stop presenting work on genre and text as if it were in opposition to the practice hammered out in classrooms where attention was paid first to pupils' learning and to a wider sense of culture, and give space for the development of ideas.

Some while ago, I undertook small scale research in several Hackney classrooms, with a view to pinning down how teachers institutionalised concerns for language used in learning in inner city, multicultural settings. I draw on this work in what follows (Burgess, 1983). My premise was that patterns of classroom organisation would help to determine opportunities for using language and would in turn constrain the forms of writing that became available. I had a theoretical interest in this, in re-locating concentrations on language and learning, which had been formed through studying developmental processes, to the cultural and institutional sites of working classrooms.

I observed teachers pioneering a practice that aimed to foster the content, and the thinking, of young people in using language, while also recognising, and examining, cultural issues in literacy within this multi-lingual setting. Such work rested on several principles. Teachers aimed to build their classrooms as communities of learners, from the culture and the experience of the group. There was recognition that learning took place over time, and not just through single lessons. Pupils were encouraged to work at moments of learning both prospectively and retrospectively. Through the intervention of the teacher classroom moments would be worked on, transformed to enterprises, and given significance in the group and at the same time to individuals. Then, retrospectively, these were re-visited and re-examined. In this manner, classrooms became the sites of an unfolding history.

To take just one example, in a lesson early in the year, groups of London Caribbean boys met a poem written in Creole, in the course of leafing through an anthology that a teacher had carefully introduced into the class's reading boxes taken out for sustained reading. Things began to happen, as a consequence. A reading was developed

34

by some. Debates about Creole were begun by others. A poem on Jamaica was written by someone else. Later in the year, a story was read, which balanced Standard English narrative with patois dialogue. The teacher worked between these moments, fostering their potential for learning. Loosely, indirectly and unthreateningly, earlier conversations, reading and writing were recalled, with the teacher helping pupils to make links between the contributions of individuals and the collective memory of the group.

Writing was made real and active and significant in such a way of working, through the teacher's work with individual intentions, building and supporting these, and helping pupils to transform them. Joint ways of working and collective interests were also built within this pattern, as teachers worked between the group and individuals. There was plenty of instruction. This was of various kinds and was operated at different levels. In part, instruction came through formation of the collective culture of the group, and through the expectations established in a way of working, as well as through explicit direction. A lot of teacher time was spent reflecting back with pupils on the significance of what was happening, re-visiting and re-evaluating earlier moments in the class's history.

It is instructive to look at recent methodologies arising from the literacy framework against this background, and at recent commentary on ways to improve young people's writing that the literacy strategy offers (Barton, 2001; Myhill, 2001). As such writers note, there is no necessary stand-off between practices that have been formed round concentration on process and on learning and understandings based on teaching about text; and much can be gained from more explicit attention to the forms of language. At the same time, it will be necessary to work for synthesis. There needs to be commitment to retain the richness of the principles that have underpinned effective English work, as well as advocacy for new approaches.

The focus of my argument so far has been the meeting between different research traditions, which has arisen from a new emphasis on text, within the more directive order of the national curriculum, the literacy hour and strategies for Key Stage 3. I have posed the need for synthesis. I have emphasised maintaining the richness of perspectives, and of practice, which have been central in forming post-war English teaching, as well as seeking to incorporate new emphases. It will be apparent that the argument assumes the creativity of teachers and corresponding recognition of their professional contribution. I have set out from the premise that the quality of the literacy strategy that the nation actually gets will rest on the initiatives of teachers and on the quality that teachers bring to implementing frameworks and objectives. What I have not done within this argument is to address the changing conditions of teachers' work, setting to one side issues that should arguably also be threaded into a consideration of English teaching's future. I want to argue in closing for attention to these longer-term issues, amongst those who work in English teaching, in our separate work places, and within curriculum movements such as NATE.

There is a well-known comment of James Britton's, where he was seeking to describe the special focus of teacher's thinking in relation to the findings of research. 'Development', he wrote, 'is a two-way process; the practitioner does not merely *apply*; he must reformulate from the general starting points supplied by research and arrive at new ends – new not only to him but new in the sense that they are not a part of the research findings, being a discovery of a different order' (1982b). Britton, it will be recalled, worked for much of his career as a tutor of English 'methods' in a university setting, where fundamental (foundational) disciplines were the senior partner. Writing at this point about relations between research and teaching and develop-ment, here as elsewhere, he stresses the active nature of practitioners' development of ideas, rejecting calls on teachers simply to apply the findings of research. I quote the passage now to draw attention to a dilemma seeded in it. The emphasis on 'reformulation' and on 'discovery of a different order' still seems to offer an appropriate, moving description, to be coveted for teaching. At the same time, the vision that Britton starts from here rests on twin assumptions of respect for the enquiries of research and for the judgements and discoveries made by teachers in their professional sphere, which now feel very different.

It would require a longer argument to set out on an inventory of change. Plainly, included in such a list would be the coming of the national curriculum, together with the regulation of its delivery. As important, courses of initial training have been made the subject of new standards, with specific curricula for core subjects. There are changed conditions for professional development. The coming of new national strategies such as that for Key Stage 3 form part of an agenda of continuous improvement, driven by the state, and linked to target setting by schools and to monitoring and self-evaluation. We may note that teachers have available now, as they did not at the time that Britton thought and wrote, the supports, as well as the constraints, of governments that want to play an active role in guiding the work of schools and classrooms. The upshot of such change, however, has not been just to give the politicians the levers and controls they wanted in order to drive up standards. It has also re-described the professionalism of teachers, curbing aspirations to autonomy and self-regulation, within an externally evaluative and regulated system, driven by an active centre, setting national priorities for performance and development.

Within our present discussion about writing, can more be envisaged strategically for English than either seeking to preserve knowledge, skills and values that have been powerful and/or working productively with the opportunities provided by national, government initiatives? Both courses of action seem necessary and important. Confronted with a more directive teaching culture, it is plainly vital to ask what English teachers most want to preserve. It seems equally clear that English teachers should exploit what is valuable in the present literacy initiative, and the English framework, building on its flexibility, mediating it productively for young people. While remaining properly critical, and self-critical, this does not have to be a negative undertaking. But neither step, of itself, puts down markers for the future development of teaching, unless it is also seen strategically. As I have suggested elsewhere (2001), the possibility that arises beyond responses of this kind is for a longer-term project, motivated from within the English teaching world. This would seek co-ordination of existing lines in English teaching with the aim to construct a new professionalism within the changed conditions of teachers' work.

The steps toward such a reformulated professionalism would not be easy. To make a start, what might be needed is re-thinking how to set directions from *within* the English teaching community that would meet, and go beyond, legitimate demands within the new professionalism that presently form part of external regulation. There is need for ownership from inside English teaching of public requirements for transparency of practice and for accountability, together with responsiveness to equality agendas and to democratic values. As important, there are more specific objects for development, where NATE might play a co-ordinating role. These include attention to professional development and to formulating requirements for courses and for practice to accompany national moves to focused training in areas of government priority. Research is needed into the development of teachers' skills and values and understandings. As well as national directions, there is need for the interpretation of government initiatives *with* as well as *to* communities, and for developments at local level.

There seem to me then two routes forward in relation to the question of this pamphlet: what is worth fighting for in English teaching? One is to reflect on what we want to keep from earlier research and from classroom practices, within present debates concerning principle. Another is to look strategically at how to build a new professionalism in a culture of teaching that has been fundamentally changed. The second route may raise more difficult questions, and they are ones that need a wide-ranging and many-sided discussion. But they are questions necessary to a firmer purchase on the future.

References

Barton, G. (2001) 'Positive Pen Power', *TES, English Curriculum Special [Summer 2001]*: 8–9

Britton, J. (1982b) 'A note on teaching, research and development' in G. Pradl (ed.) *Prospect and Retrospect: Selected Essays of James Britton*, London: Heinemann

Burgess, T. (1983) 'Diverse Melodies' in Miller, J. (ed.) *Eccentric Propositions*, London: Routledge

Burgess, T. (2001) Review of John Furlong et al. Teacher Education in Transition. Reforming Professionalism in *Changing English*, Vol. 8, 2: 203–208

Furlong, J. et al. (2000) *Teacher Education in Transition. Re-forming Professionalism*, Buckingham/Philadelphia: Open University Press

Graves, D. (1986) *Writing: Teachers and Children at Work*, New Hampshire: Heinemann

Heath, S.B. (1983) *Ways with Words: Language and Life in Communities and Classrooms*, Cambridge: Cambridge University Press

Hymes, D. (1972) Introduction in Courtney Cazden (ed.) *Functions of Language in the Classroom*, New York: Teachers College Press

Gregory, E. and Williams, A. (2000) *City Literacies. Learning to read across generations*, London and New York: Routledge

Halliday, M. (1985) *An Introduction to Functional Grammar*, London: Arnold

HMSO (1988) *Report of the Committee of Inquiry into the Teaching of English Language (The Kingman Report)*

Minns, H. (1990) *Read it to Me Now!*, London: Virago Press

Myhill, D. (2001) 'Why shaping and crafting matter', *The Secondary English Magazine*, Vol. 5, 1: 15–19

Contributors

Tony Burgess is a reader at London University's Institute of Education, with particular interests in writing, language diversity and English teaching's history.

Carol Fox has worked in teacher education since 1984, having previously taught English in London schools. Her interests include children's literature, narrative and the development of spoken language.

Joan Goody was Head of English in a multi-ethnic, inner London comprehensive for many years. She established and chaired NATE's multicultural committee and co-ordinated the Arts Council funded international literature project.

Perspectives on English Teaching aims to inform debates and provoke discussion about English and English teaching. NATE will publish two titles each year and all members are encouraged to contribute. If you have a proposal for a title in this series – either as sole author or with others – please contact the Series Editor, Viv Ellis, in the first instance.